M000210467

Creating Your Own Spells

Monique Joiner Siedlak

OSHUN
PUBLICATIONS

Printed in the United States of America

Second Edition 2018

ISBN-13: 978-1-948834-07-0

ISBN-10: 1-948834-07-3

www.oshunpublications.com

Disclaimer

All the material contained in this book is provided for educational and informational purposes only. No responsibility can be taken for any results or outcomes resulting from the use of this material. While every attempt has been made to provide information that is both accurate and effective, the author does not assume any responsibility for the accuracy or use/misuse of this information.

Cover design by Monique Joiner Siedlak

Cover image by Pixabay.com

Logo design by Monique Joiner Siedlak

Logo image by Pixabay.com

Other Books in the Series

Wiccan Basics

Candle Magick

Wiccan Spells

Love Spells

Abundance Spells

Hoodoo

Herb Magick

Seven African Powers

Moon Magick

Cooking for the Orishas

Sign up at http://mojosiedlak.com for my newsletter and receive a free book.

Table of Contents

About This Book

Without question, there is nothing wrong with working spells from other individuals. It's how most Wiccan first began on the path. If you check the bookstores, online as well as brick and mortar, you will find tons of them. Even I wrote a few of those books. It possible that a time may come you cannot locate a book with what you are looking for. You may find that some spells in their wording, may not resonate with you and you might want to use your own.

There are no fixed rules on how to create spells and what one individual considers right may not work as well for others. It may possibly take some time experimenting and practicing to discover what works best for you, particularly if you do not possess very much skill with spell work.

Successfully accomplishing a spell is a skill that comes in relation to practice. The better you are at performing with magickal energy, the better your results will be. The more you know the spell, the more effective it will be.

When creating your own spells, several elements can help you in the process. These elements are:

8/ CREATING YOUR OWN SPELLS

1. Your intent and reason for the spell

2. Collecting suitable supplies

3. Meditation, an image or a chant to focus on

4. When you will perform the spell

5. Casting the spell itself

6. Evaluating and recording the spell.

Whatever your reason for wanting to create your own spells, it is not as difficult as you may think. You do not have to a creative type of person. All you need to do is implement a few things and voila! You will have a spell written for you, by you.

Good luck and enjoy!

Chapter One
Getting Ready

Prepare Yourself

The first step in any magickal work is to get yourself ready.
You must first question yourself if a spell is in fact necessary.
Can it be solved in a mundane way? Have you exhausted all
avenues before using magick? You cannot expect to say,
"Abracadabra" and it's done. If only it was that easy.

This is when you would purify and cleanse yourself. Ever
since the beginning of time individuals has used fasting or
abstinence for this purpose. You can do just a
straightforward bathing ritual. The main goal while cleansing
yourself must be to clear your mind, calm your body and your
spirit, and becoming ready for the magick.

Add a hand full of sea salt to get yourself ready a nice
relaxing bath. Light a few candles, turn off the lights and
release. Free your mind of the garbage you have collected up
throughout the day. See in your mind's eye the bathwater

carrying away all the negativity from you. It is imperative that your mind is at ease and positive prior to any spell working.

Make ready your thoughts and avoid the indecision or fear in your mind. Your hesitant mind can be an obstacle to achieving success with your magickal experience and you must overcome it.

On the day leading up to the spell you may want to eat light or fast, meditate and center yourself, take a cleansing bath or purify yourself in some way.

A Few Things You Can Do Everyday

Drink water. Water conducts energy and is adaptable. It changes contingent on what the intention or offering is. It gives your clarity of the mind and can help you feel at ease.

An element of physical energy, exercise can help you focus on your intention.

Believe it or not, meditation is essential. You must learn to silence the mind and focus at will.

Do some type magick every day. It does not have to be an intricate spell. You can simply focus on something; ask for something to come about with a small mantra, chant or song. Keep an eye out for the outcome. This will develop your bond the energy of the Goddess and to the Universe.

To be successful, you want to plan. The first detail required is for you to come to a decision of precisely what it is that you desire and how you will get it by this spell. What are you expecting to be the result? In what way will it happen exactly?

Be very in depth and write down the result exactly how it will come about. Shut your eyes and visualize the outcome, be very accurate and thorough as possible. This assists and expresses the real intention of the spell and helps establish the movement of the Universe giving you what you ask for in action.

Prepare Your Space

Before you start any spell or ritual, you must cleanse and clear the area where the undertaking is to be performed. This is particularly correct as you first bless your sacred space. You ought to cleanse this space every time you make use of this space or start a ritual. However, you will find that these later efforts will all be affected by how you first set the intent and use of energy in this space for the first time.

The notion is to get rid of any unwelcome energy that may affect or hinder with your spiritual experience. For your ritual area, the clearing and cleansing portion should be performed prior to each action. This can be achieved in just a couple of minutes. You actually do not need to build this into a most important effort. The most general habit is as you say a spell, prayer, or burn incense while moving in a clockwise path to remove the negative and unwanted energies. Try to work in every corner, under the furniture. At that point, walk around the space a second time to place a protective shield to keep those negative energies from re-entering your space.

Set up your tools and supplies. Set up your altar. You can use whatever you wish to decorate your altar, however, try to stay away from fabricated materials. For the actual altar, you can use a small wooden table. You can display your God pictures/statuettes on the right, and the Goddess images on the left.

Simply follow this manner any time you want to cast a spell, customizing your altar for that particular spell. Select the colors of the candles, charms, stones, and figures, to correspond with the energy you are attempting to encourage, if the altar is a depiction of you and what you are trying to achieve.

Chapter Two

What Is Your Goal?

The most significant ingredient of any spell is your intent.
What is it you hope to bring about? Are you considering
bringing love into your life? Wishing for prosperity?
Attempting to find a better job? What is the precise goal of
the spell? Whatever it might be, make sure you are clear on
what it is you want.

When you're going to cast a spell you need to be mentally
fixed on what you desire to occur. You ought to undoubtedly
meditate before even make an attempt to cast a spell. If you
don't meditate your mind may be running on with unplanned
thoughts. A clear mind is a very crucial step. You have to put
all of your emotions into the spell.

The intent of your spell should be written down or stated
aloud. "I will get that promotion." Be specific with your spell.
Do not just cast a wish spell or just make things easy spell.
What is that you actually need? Nail it down to the details.
Know the job you want. See it, feel it. "I will have the ideal

man/woman." See them. Image how things will be or write it down. For me, I knew exactly the type of man I was looking for. One particular movie had exactly what I wanted. I watched it every day. I could feel myself having such a relationship. I met my husband, three months later.

If you can't declare what you desire in a few words, you're probably not focused sufficiently. You need to truly feel the spell working. Believing what is true in the spell. When casting your spell visualize it working. Maintain that feeling until you believe you have raised enough energy and focused it.

Break it down into smaller aims when your overall goal is complicated. Just imagine about how many steps, parts or changes it would require to achieve your intent. Do a particular spell for each one of those instead of one big spell to try to change everything at one time.

The explanation why a spell may work or does not work continues to be open to debate. The simple principle is that a spell works by focusing and directing your mind on your specified intention. Your personal energy as well as the energy of the natural elements that you use in your spell assists to focus your mind on the intended goal and manifest in your reality.

Chapter Three
What Items Do You Need?

Just like cooking, spells can be considered as a sort of recipe. In the instance of spells the more knowledge and experience you achieve the better the result will be. This knowledge signifies not only understanding how to construct and cast a spell, but also in addition to studying about which deities, crystals, colors, herbs, days and other pertinent items that will be best matched to the type of spell you wish to create.

When you are casting spells, you should have the right items or tools to use. You will find that many tools characterize many purposes. The correct purposes will add more power when you are casting your spell. For instance, if I were casting a money spell, I would more than likely use a green candle because it represents money. Therefore, the tools you use in fact matter. If you do not use any type of tool, you may have a less chance of your spells working.

So, what items do you need? Every herb, color, gemstone has its own properties. For example, if you were doing a spell for money, you would use herbs such Basil, Cinnamon, Clove or Patchouli. The oils could be Cedar, Clove, or Patchouli. Citrine, Green Aventurine or Jade would be your gemstones. Of course the color green. As in green for money. Green candles, green sachet. Perform on a Thursday or Sunday. For protection, try Aloe, Basil, and Garlic. Amber, Garnet, Turquoise. Colors blue, white on a Thursday

Will your spell require herbs, candles, stones? Do not get bogged down in all the details. You could use play money for money spells. I actually have 1,000-dollar bills printed in wallet size for when I perform money spells. There are Beetles also, being my dream car, to protect her. When you are creating a spell, bear in mind that magick depends greatly on representation. Everything is simply not so literal.

If you are drawn to a certain item while you are performing on a spell or get a sensation from it that it could work well, it is acceptable to go with that sense. Your own instincts and gut feelings are a very significant portion of creating your own spells as well as any magick or witchcraft in general so by no means feel afraid to follow these. Hang onto thorough notes of your spells and other magickal work in the Book of Shadows or a journal so that you can turn to these in the future and learn from any successes and errors. You will be able to build your own personal list of correspondences over time, and may decide to work from these alone or in combination with material from other resources.

Remember, write everything down, make a list and check it twice.

Chapter Four
Timing Is Important, Sometimes

In some traditions, the moon's phase is essential, although in others it is not important. When you want to bring things to you, for increase or gain, you should start when the moon is waxing. This is from the New Moon to the Full Moon. When working for banishing, decreasing or sending something away, you should start when the moon is waning. This time would be the Full Moon to the New Moon. The greatest moon energy happens with the Full Moon. This is the most powerful phase for magickal workings followed by the New Moon.

Your spells are usually worked on the day or days where it would be more effective. For example, for divination and healing magick, Monday would be the day to perform. Sunday, using the energy of the sun would be the best time for healing and success, to obtain goals.

The time of the day for spells will also play a part. Midday is the best time for spells requiring the full energy of the Sun.

18/ CREATING YOUR OWN SPELLS

To bring in new energies such as a new job or relationship, Dawn, the start of a new day, is the time to begin.

It may possibly be that you believe a particular day of the week is best for the working, or even a specific time of the day. Do not overwhelm yourself with the aspects of the spell if you are an individual who feels self-assured performing magick on a moment's notice, with no worry about the timing, then any time is an excellent time.

You will find that the Moon's phase comes into play a great deal when talking about spell casting. The Moon increases your energy so you have more of a possibility of your spell working; however, it depends on your spell. Identifying the correct period to cast your spell is key as well. Set your intention when to cast your spell.

Chapter Five
Your Wording

Writing your own spell is not difficult. It helps you to not
only distinguish your spell, but to focus on it. Do you know
what words you will use? Do you plan to chant? Will it be
vocalized during your spell or murmured under your breath?
Are you going to recite something ceremonial and
authoritative, calling upon the Gods/Goddesses for support?
Perhaps it will be the type where you simply meditate on.
Keep in mind, there is power in your words, so choose them
wisely.

Here's plus, if you did not know, there are rhyming
dictionaries available. I have one that sits on my shelf with
my other books. I like my spells to rhyme. They usually have
a beat to them and they seem to have more power to them. If
you ever are stuck on what to rhyme a word with, it is totally
worth it.

Once you have chosen your deity and elements, you are ready
to write an incantation. You want to invoke a goddess, god or

element. Then you want to state clearly, what it is that you desire. Finally, you want to leave it open to the universe to give you what is right for you. You do not want to control the outcome or a particular person.

Write your spell. Review it, fine-tune it, adjust it and familiarize yourself with it well. You don't have to memorize it, you can if you want, but you should really be familiar with the steps and what you have to say so it flows naturally. Even though you might be using notes, you should not be faltering over them in view of the fact that you barely glimpsed at them.

Chapter Six
Grounding Power

Grounding is a vital two parts of understanding how to practice magick in a healthy and harmless way. This is similar to the process of grounding an electrical circuit. In essence, if an item is positively charged, electrons transfers from the ground into the item, as well, if an item is charged negatively, the act of grounding lets left over electrons to transfer from the item into the ground. It's a process of equalizing and balancing the movement of energy.

The first part is when you begin a spell or ritual. You want to focus on whatever you will be performing. In this circumstance, grounding, centering helps to provide you the energy for the undertaking ahead, and helps you to block out interruptions so that you can give all your focus to the magickal work.

To begin, sit up straight sitting with your legs crossed. Place your palms on your knees and relax your body. Closing your eyes, take deep, long breaths, and slow your breathing.

After you have been calmed, picture yourself as a tree. You are sending roots out of your feet into the Earth and your arms are becoming long branches, with leaves as fingers.

Let go all your negative thoughts, anxieties, fears, and leftover energy. Drive them down into your roots.

Once you have completed that, with your branches and leaves, draw in energy, and feel the positive feelings flowing through your body/trunk, and into your body, mind, and spirit, to balance your energy. Keep forcing the negative energy down through your roots; the energy system is a never-ending cycle.

Feel the power flow in your system. Visualize the power collecting it into a ball of strong energy at your heart. Immerse yourself and relax in the beauty of the natural energy before slowly opening your eyes. Take another few deep breaths, at that time channel that light, and work into your magick.

The second is toward the end of your spell or ritual when you have created the magickal energy and focused it into your magick. In this instance, grounding and centering helps to channel any residual, surplus energy out of your body, allowing it to flow into the ground. This is similar to cooling-down after an intense exercising activity, grounding returns you to a normal level of energy.

Now is the moment to give thanks and say goodbye to any deity or power you decided to invite into your circle.

Chapter Seven
Casting the Spell

Once you are all set to start your spell, it's time to cast a circle of energy to create a sacred area and to keep out negativity.

Once you have setup the physical circle borders, be sure all of the objects you will need for the spell are in the circle or on your altar. You do not want to exit your circle once you have begun.

Make sure you represent each of the four elements in the four quarters of your circle or at least make sure they are represented on your altar. My altar has four 2 ounce shot glasses containing nothing for Air, salt for Earth, water for Water and a candle for Fire.

Using your athame, finger, or wand to move clockwise near the inside perimeter of your circle three times, as you repeat:

"As I cast this circle 3 times about, I will keep bad energy out."

You can chant this or create your own. Keep in mind; you are creating your own spell.

Make your request to any deities or spirits you want to help you with the spell. Invite them to protect the circle in addition.

You can grasp an anointed candle with the corresponding oil in your hands.

You will need to anoint the candle starting from the bottom, working your way up to the top if you are drawing something or increasing something. For removing or reducing something, you will then want to anoint from the top of the candle, down to the bottom.

Holding the candle in your hands, start seeing in your mind's eye the outcome you want to create. Do not just visualize it in your mind, but also genuinely get into the vision and experience the enjoyment and pleasure you will feel when your intention becomes reality. The more passion and energy you can imbue into the candle, the more strength your spell will have.

This is your charging process. There is nothing to be concerned about if your hands become warm. It is your energy flowing from your hands and into the candle, to charge it with your intention.

You may then light another candle if you are using more than one along with incense, continuing your visualization process. You want to infuse as much energy and emotion into your spell as you can.

If workable, let the candle to burn down all the way and end on its own. If you're no table to, you can extinguish it and re-ignite it as often as you need to until it burns all the way down. You do not want to blow out your candles. It has been thought to scatter the energies of your spell.

Now that you have completed your spell, it's time to open your circle. This is completed by walking three times counterclockwise as you repeat:

"As I walk 3 times about opening my circle, I release the energy."

Once again, you can chant this or create your own.

Your spell is now completed. Make sure to thank any deities or spirits you invited through the spell and thank the elements.

Once your spell is completed, simply give thankfulness to the Goddess/God/Universe for the blessings that you know are in their direction to you and close the circle.

Chapter Eight
Recording Spells

The most significant thing when performing spells and even rituals is to record your experiences. It can be done right in your Book of Shadows. This is so that you have details of your magickal work. Once you do your workings, write everything that you can remember of that day. The more facts you write down the better. Even though it may not seem significant now, it can turn out to be very important afterwards. It is useful to have a record on your spells, as most magick you perform will not manifest right away. It may take time for it to come to fruition.

Here are a few things you should answer when recording your spell:

1. What type of spell did you perform?

2. Where did you get the information used?

3. Were you suffering from sickness, worry or indecision?

4. What was the date, time, astrological phase when performed?

5. Were deities summoned during the planning and or use?

6. What are the step-by-step directions for preparation and or use?

7. Why are you doing this spell?

8. What ingredients and supplies were used?

9. Was this an indoor or outdoor spell?

10. What were your results? Did it work well? What could have been different?

11. What are your thoughts and feelings after the spell?

Chapter Nine
Spell Evaluation

A very important step after working the spell comes the assessment process. As soon as you can, sit down and take observations about just how well the process worked. Did everything go as intended? If you had to repeat the spell, would you modify anything? When completing your notes, store them away for future purpose. Certain magickal traditions warn against speaking about spell work until a certain period of time has occurred, thinking that to speak of the magick is to discharge some of its contained energy. Abide by these traditions as needed by your own practices, but be certain to do your own written assessment for your eyes only. Go back to it again when time has passed, inserting a note about how well the spell worked throughout the weeks or months.

Like with any spell work, discard of all residue of the process when your working is completed. Get rid of materials using the proper basic means such as burning them, releasing them in water or burying them in the earth. Cleanse and keep your magickal tools and replace any used or depleted items. You do not want to need an item just to realize you forgot you finished it in the course of your last spell.

Chapter Ten
Conclusion

In spite of this being a straightforward and basic manner of examining a spell's creation, it does work efficiently. Create notes in your Book of Shadows or keep a journal in the course of the spell creation period, I personally keep track of my results as they start to manifest in a separate journal. You may wish to do so as well.

A number of individuals say that within 28 days, if a spell has not started to manifest you might want to stop and go back to the spell. You may need to figure out what adjustments might need to be changed.

If your spell did not work as you anticipated, the first thing you possibly will want to take into account is whether the spell really failed. Was there enough time given for your manifestation? Generally, it can take a spell up to 30 days or a full moon cycle to manifest. IT may even take up to 90 days or three moon cycles. Are you are rushing it by second-guessing yourself?

You have to examine if it could be it did achieve something, but not in the manner you wanted. Did you perform an abundance spell and later on finding a dollar in the wash or received a 10 dollar gift card in the mail? Were you upset at the amount or did you treat it as if it was the best thing ever? It may not have been the outcome you sought, but that could very well have been the outcome.

It could be your goal wasn't sensible. Just because magick is real doesn't mean everything is in the sphere of probability is. Everything real also has real limits. There are no exceptions with Magick. If you're casting spells for the improbable, it will take much more skill and effort. You are wasting your time if you're casting spells for the impossible, like changing your height, becoming a dragon or even a cat. It will not happen. Ever.

To cast a spell correctly, it is essential to know what you are doing. If you haven't learned the basic concepts, exactly how do you know the spell you wrote is a decent one? How do you know it doesn't have elemental mistakes?

When you're casting spells you want to remain positive. You will want to avoid negative words similar to don't, can't, or won't. Phrase everything in the constructive, with an effective, forceful language.

Your mind is the most important instrument in your spell work. The more adept your instrument is, the better your results will be. Many individuals don't like meditating, but how do you expect to put the necessary intent into a spell if you can't focus? Exactly how do you believe to adjust your state of awareness when you can't even control your own mind?

Once more, if this is your problem, it may well be best to go back to the beginning with a good meditation routine. If you want to perform magick, you can do this. It's a practice you might really want to be skilled at doing and you may actually enjoy it.

Just because you use magick, does not mean your work is done. If you perform a spell to aid in good health, is eating the wrong food going to help or hinder? If you want to meet the love of your life, then staying home watching the latest reality television show is not going to get you too far. It is all common sense.

There is no correct way to doing things. The Goddess and God recognize you as a beginner and want to help you while you are learning. Your spells are built with you in addition to your energy. Only you are responsible for it, and it ought to be yours from conception to execution. Keep in mind that any form of influence over someone else deems a negative action. This is also true for spells with good intentions. You will find that the Universe has its own way of doing things. Simply, word your spell correctly.

Appendix One
Day of the Week Magickal Correspondences

Since the numerous gods control them, each day of the week creates an energy that is the best type of magickal working. The following is a list, which despite the fact is not completely comprehensive; here are a number of ideas of when to execute your spells.

Sunday

Gender: Masculine

Color: Yellow

Planet: Sun

Element: Fire

Incenses: Cedar, Cinnamon Frankincense, Lemon, Sun Oil

Energies: Ambition, Goals, Career, Children, Fun, Health, Law, Success, Personal Finances, Promotion, Selling, Volunteers, Civic Services

Monday

Gender: Feminine

Color: White

Planet: Moon

Element: Water

Incenses: Honeysuckle, Jasmine, Moon Oil, Sandalwood, Wormwood

Energies: Astrology, Children, Dreams/Astral Travel, Emotions, Imagination, Initiation, Magick, New-Age Pursuits, Psychology, Reincarnation, Religion, Short Trips, Spirituality

Tuesday

Gender: Masculine

Color: Red

Planet: Mars

Element: Fire

Incenses: Basil, Black Pepper, Dragon's Blood, Ginger, Patchouli

Energies: Aggression, Business, Beginnings, Combat, Confrontation, Courage, Passion, Partnerships, Sex

Wednesday

Gender: Masculine

Color: Purple

Planet: Mercury

Element: Air

Incenses: Eucalyptus, Mercury Oil, Jasmine, Lavender, Sweet Pea

Energies: Astrology, Communication, Computers, Correspondence, Editing, Healing, Hiring, Legal Appointments, Messages, Music, Signing Contracts, Students, Writing

Thursday

Gender: Masculine

Color: Green

Planet: Jupiter

Element: Earth

Incenses: Cinnamon, Clove, Jupiter Oil, Musk, Nutmeg, Oak Moss, Patchouli, Sage

Energies: Business, Charity, College, Expansion, Gambling, Growth, Law, Luck, Material Wealth, Publishing, Researching, Self-Improvement

Friday

Gender: Feminine

Color: Blue

Planet: Venus

Element: Water

Incenses: Cardamom, Rose, Saffron, Sandalwood, Strawberry, Vanilla, Venus Oil, Yarrow

Energies: Affection, Artists, Beauty, Courtship, Friendships, Gardening, Marriage, Music, Partners, Poetry, Relationships, Romantic Love, Shopping, Social Activity

Saturday

Gender: Feminine

Color: Black

Planet: Saturn

Element: Fire, Earth

Incenses: Cypress, Myrrh, Patchouli, Saturn Oil

Energies: Binding, Debts, Financing, Hard Work, Housing, Justice, Karma, Limits, Manifestation, Obstacles, Plumbing, Protection, Transformation

Appendix Two
Herbs of the Zodiac

The Zodiac Sign Capricorn falls between the dates of December 22nd to January 19th. This zodiac's herb includes Caraway, Chamomile, Comfrey, Jasmine Marjoram, Rosemary Slippery Elm, Tarragon, and Thyme.

The Zodiac Sign Aquarius falls between the dates of January 20st to February 18th. This zodiac's herb includes Comfrey, Fennel, Frankincense, Myrrh, Peppermint Rosemary, Sandalwood Valerian, and Violet.

The Zodiac Sign Pisces falls between the dates of February 19th to March 20th. This zodiac's herb includes Basil, Borage, Hyacinth, Irish Moss, Lemon Balm, Lovage, Sage, and Willow.

The Zodiac Sign Aries falls between the dates of March 21st to April 19th. This zodiac's herb includes Angelical Root, Basil Chervil, Garlic, Geranium, Hemp, Marjoram, Mustard Seed and Wormwood.

The Zodiac Sign Taurus falls between the dates of April 20th to May 20th. This zodiac's herb includes Catnip Cedar, Colts Foot, Dandelion, Marsh Mallow Mint Patchouli, Sage, Thyme and Violet.

The Zodiac Sign Gemini falls between the dates of May 21st to June 20th. This zodiac's herb includes Anise, Caraway Seed, Dill, Lavender, Mandrake, Marjoram, Mugwort, Parsley, Vervain, and Wormwood.

The Zodiac Sign Cancer falls between the dates of June 21st to July 22nd. This zodiac's herb includes Aloe, Apple, Bay, Catnip, Geranium Lemon Verbena, Marigold Parsley, and Sage.

The Zodiac Sign Leo falls between the dates of July 23rd to August 22nd. This zodiac's herb includes Anise, Bay Leaves, Chamomile Clove Dill, Eyebright, Lemon Balm, Mint, Oak, Sunflower, and Tarragon.

The Zodiac Sign Virgo falls between the dates of August 23rd to September 22nd. This zodiac's herb includes Caraway Cyprus Dill, Fennel Seed, Horehound, Marjoram, Mint, Skullcap and Valerian.

The Zodiac Sign Libra falls between the dates of September 23rd to October 22nd. This zodiac's herb includes Bergamot Catnip Elderberry, Lemon Verbena, Penny Royal, St. John's Wort and Thyme.

The Zodiac Sign Scorpio falls between the dates of October 23rd to November 21st. This zodiac's herb includes Ash, Basil, Catnip, Coriander, Hops, Horehound, Nettle, Sage, and Sarsaparilla.

The Zodiac Sign Sagittarius falls between the dates of November 22nd to December 21st. This zodiac's herb includes Basil Borage, Burdock, Chervil, Red Clover, Saffron Sage, St. John's Wort and Tobacco.

*Note: The dates may vary by a day or two.

Appendix Three
Magickal Color Correspondence

Red: Energy, Excitement, Power, Passion, Protection, Overcomes Fear, Strength

Pink: Spiritual Love, Romance, Success, Attraction, Compassion, Understanding, Gentleness, Friendship, Forgiveness Self-Love, Self-Respect Heals Broken Hearts, Overcomes Conflict

Orange: Can be substituted for Gold. Success, Emotional Clarity, Control, Happiness, Pleasure, Attracts Luck and Money, Enthusiasm Energy, Hopefulness, Confidence

Yellow: Attraction, Success, Drawing, Communicating, Studying, Memory, Clear Thinking, Decision Making, Confidence

Green: Fertility, Better Business, Creative Ideas, Money, Employment, Rewards, Good Luck, Earth, Plants, Growing

Blue: Harmony, Loyalty, Astral Travel, Tranquility, Psychic Ability, Integrity, Truth, Meditation, Kindness, Knowledge,

Reduces Excess Energy, Relieves Anxiety and Stress, Helps Insomnia

Purple: Blue And Red Energy, Competition, Achieve Work Success, Wealth, Dignity, Control, Respect, Honor, Obedience, Overcome Odds, Command, Court Cases, Awareness, Victory, Blocks Negativity

White: All-Purpose Spiritual Awareness and Power. Purity, Truth, Spiritual Devotion, Cooperation, Assistance

Gold: The Sun. Success, Wealth, Wishes, Happiness

Silver: Gray Often Used For Silver. Quick Money, Gambling, Moon Magick

Gray: Neutralizes Stress, Negativity, Decreases the Impact of Mistakes, Cleanse Unwanted Energies, Break A Spell of Bad Luck, and Exorcisms

Black: Freedom from Evil, Transformation

Brown: Consistency, Fertility, Thrift, Work, Awareness, Control, Fruitful, Success in Business, Grounding, Long-Term Achievements, Growth, Determination, Planting

Appendix Four
Moon Phases

New Moon

When the moon is unseen, also called the Dark of the Moon, it is the most influencing time to cast spells relating to new beginnings. It is normally a time to seize new paths and creating new plans started on the foundation of past events. The impact of the New moon can furthermore increase your dreams and professions, so it is a beneficial time to planting the seeds of achievement. For the period of the New Moon, you will find that abundance spells, and employment spells have an improved possibility of being achieved than at other times. The New Moon is also commonly a suitable time to take a chance the future and spending currency and those who have undergone difficulties ought to take use of this indispensable phase.

Waxing Moon

The phase in the middle of the New Moon and Full Moon is the Waxing Moon. This is a distinctive period for gathering strength, development and growth. It is likewise a fitting time for arranging your magickal spells for the best favorable time, with that being the three days prior to the moon reaching full. The waxing moon helps the achievement of any actions, whether of an everyday or spiritual temperament. For pagans/witches it is a period for pursuits, approval and a time in which to improve our magickal powers and our awareness of the other world. Actually, the closer we move towards the Full moon, the greater and more ambitious are our instinctive power, which brings a new stage of mindfulness.

Full Moon

The Full Moon is the best opportunity time, particularly when it's drawing near Midnight, the witching hour. Your magical powers and inner strength will be at their greatest. If you want more love in your life, this day is the time to send your wants into the universe. The Full Moon is furthermore the best fitting time to give appreciation and to pay honor to the spirits that protect and guide you. Through this time, the outgoing characteristics of our personality begin to appear more extrovert and open towards others. Use this period intelligently and develop your spells into gratifying practices.

Waning Moon

This is the phase when the moon travels from Full to New Moon. Casting spells for doing away with trouble, defeating enemies, removing problems, and producing harm is most effective when the moon is waning. Protection spells for yourself, your loved ones, home and material possessions are best cast at this time. It is also a time when our bodies are more susceptible to cleansing, so it is a good time to cleanse yourself through the process of detoxification. This can be best accomplished by way of healing and herbal remedies. You will find that diet and exercise likewise turn out to be easier in the course of this time with the results having a tendency to last longer.

Appendix Five
Correspondences for the Elements

Air

Pentagram Position: Upper Left

Direction: East

Goddess: Aradia, Urania, Cardea, Nuit, Athena, Arianrhod

God: Enlil, Kheohera, Mercury, Hermes, Shu, Thoth

Colors: All Light Hues, Colors Found at Dawn. White, Yellow, Light Blue, Lavender, Gray

Associations: Addictions, Communication, Finding Lost Items, Freedom, Instruction, Knowledge, Study, Travel

Zodiac: Gemini, Libra, Aquarius

Tools: Athame, Sword, Censer, Incense

Type of Magick: Karma, Divination, Concentration, Wind Magick, Prophecy,

Earth

Pentagram Position: Lower Left

Direction: North

Goddess: Ceres, Demeter, Nephthys, Rhea, Rhiannon, Cerridwyn, Gaia, Persephone, Epona, Kore, Mah, Prithivi

God: Cernunnos, Adonis, Athos, Arawn, Herne, Marduk, Pan, Tammuz, Thor, Dionysus

Colors: Deep Earth Tones, Green, Brow, Black, Gold, White

Associations: Abundance, Employment, Fertility, Foundations, Grounding, Money, Prosperity, Stability

Zodiac: Taurus, Virgo, and Capricorn

Tools: Pentacle, Salt, Images, Stones, Cord Magick

Type of Magick: Gardening, Magnet Images, Stone, Knot, Binding, Money Spells, Grounding, Finding Treasures, Runes

Fire

Pentagram Position: Lower Right

Direction: South

Goddess: Brigit, Pele, Vesta, Freya, Hestia

God: Agni, Prometheus, Vulcan, Ra, Hephaestus, Horus Sekhmet, Apollo and Lugh

Colors: Red, Red-Orange, Fiery Colors, Gold, White

Associations: Anger, Authority, Banishing Negativity, Courage, Creativity, Energy, Protection, Sex, Strength

Zodiac: Aries, Leo, Sagittarius

Tools: Censer, Athame, Wand, Candles, Dagger, Herbs or Requests Burned On Paper

Type of Magick: Candle, Healing, Love Spells, Energy Work

Water

Pentagram Position: Upper Right

Direction: West

Goddess: Yemaya, Aphrodite, Venus, Epona, Isis, Mariamne, Mari, Kupala, Tiamat, Ran

God: Ea, Manannan, Dylan, Osiris, Neptune, Poseidon, Varuna

Colors: All Blue-Green-Black Hues, Corresponding To the Colors of Water, Gray, Indigo, Aquamarine, White

Associations: Dreams, Friendships, Love, Marriage, Peace, Psychic Awareness, Purification, Sleep

Zodiac: Cancer, Scorpio, Pisces

Tools: Chalice, Cauldron, Mirrors

Type of Magick: Mirror Divinations, Magnet Work, Love Magick, Lucid Dreaming, Cleansing, Protection Spells

Spirit

Pentagram Position: Upper

Direction: Center

Goddesses: The Lady, Isis

Gods: The Horned God, Akasha

Color: Purple or White, Rainbow, Black

Associations: Unification, Magic, Change, Transformation, Alchemy, Divinity

Zodiac: None

Magickal Tool: Cauldron

Type of Magick: Religious in Nature

About the Author

Born in Long Island, Monique Joiner Siedlak realized she was a Witch at the age of 12. An avid reader, her favorite genres are Horror, Science Fiction & Fantasy and Paranormal Romance, while constantly learning about the world unseen. Apparently, she has never been afraid of what goes bump into the night.

With her husband, two dogs and four cats, she now works part-time while travelling and writing.

Yoga for Menstruation Book Ten

Beautiful You Series

Creating Your Own Body Butter Book One

Creating Your Own Body Scrub Book Two

Creating Your Own Body Spray Book Three

Mojo's Self-Improvement Series

Manifesting With the Law of Attraction

Stress Management

Connect With Monique Joiner Siedlak

I really appreciate you reading my book! Please leave a review and let me know your thoughts. Here are the social media locations you can find me at:

Like my Facebook page: http://facebook.com/mojosiedlak

Follow me on Twitter: http://twitter.com/mojosiedlak

Follow me on Instagram: http://instagram.com/mojosiedlak

Follow me on Bookbub:
www.bookbub.com/authors/monique-joiner-siedlak

Subscribe to my newsletter: http://mojosiedlak.com and receive a free book!

If you enjoyed this book or found it useful I'd be very grateful if you'd post a short review on at your retailer. Your support really does make a difference and I read all the reviews personally so I can get your feedback and make this as well as the next book even better.